I0617243

Total Harmony in Hues

MOON, SARAH, Author
Total Harmony in Hues
SARAH MOON

ISBN: 979-8-9878407-3-3

QUANTITY PURCHASES: Schools, companies, professional groups, clubs, and other organizations may qualify for special terms when ordering quantities of this title.
For information, email TotalityWorkshop.com

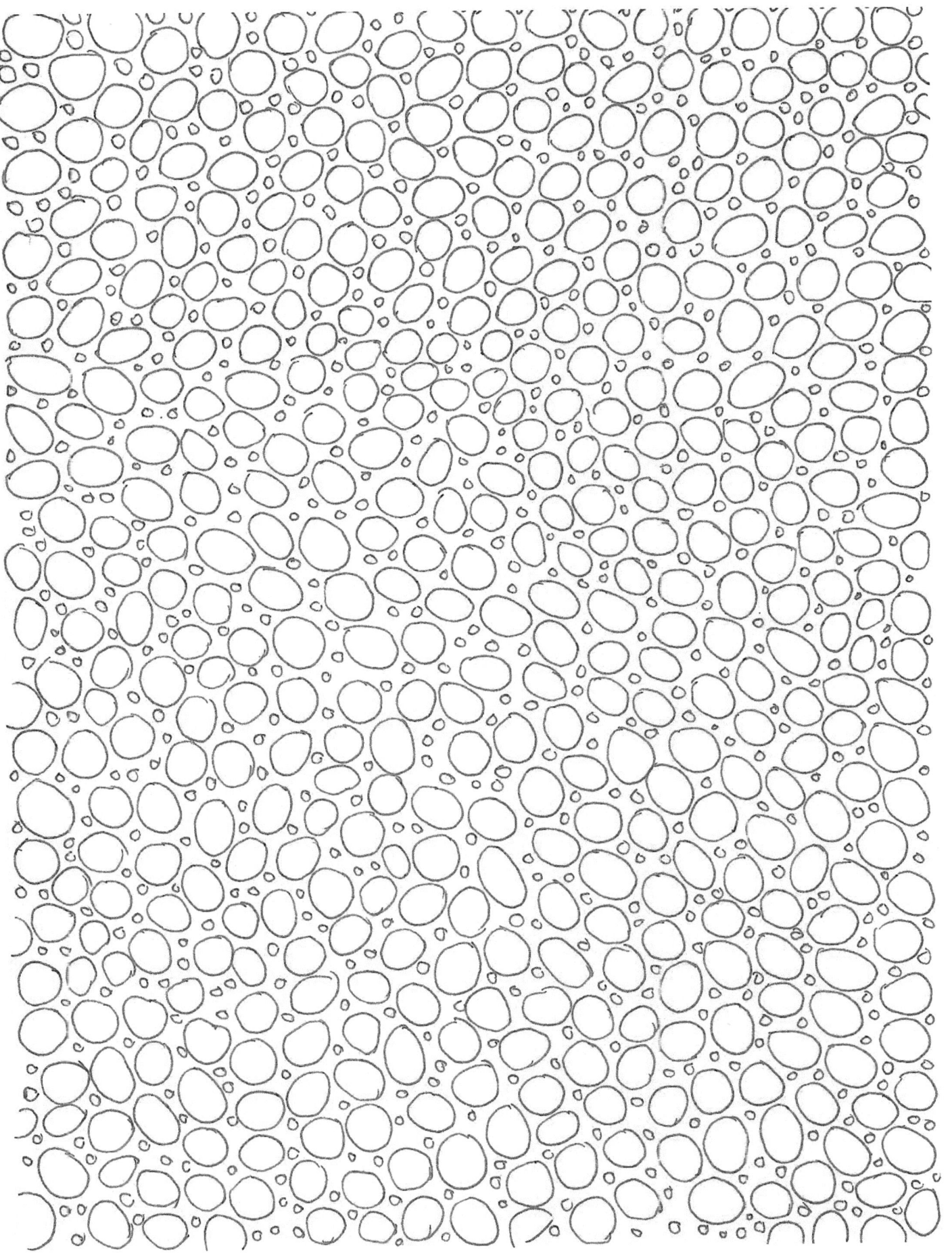

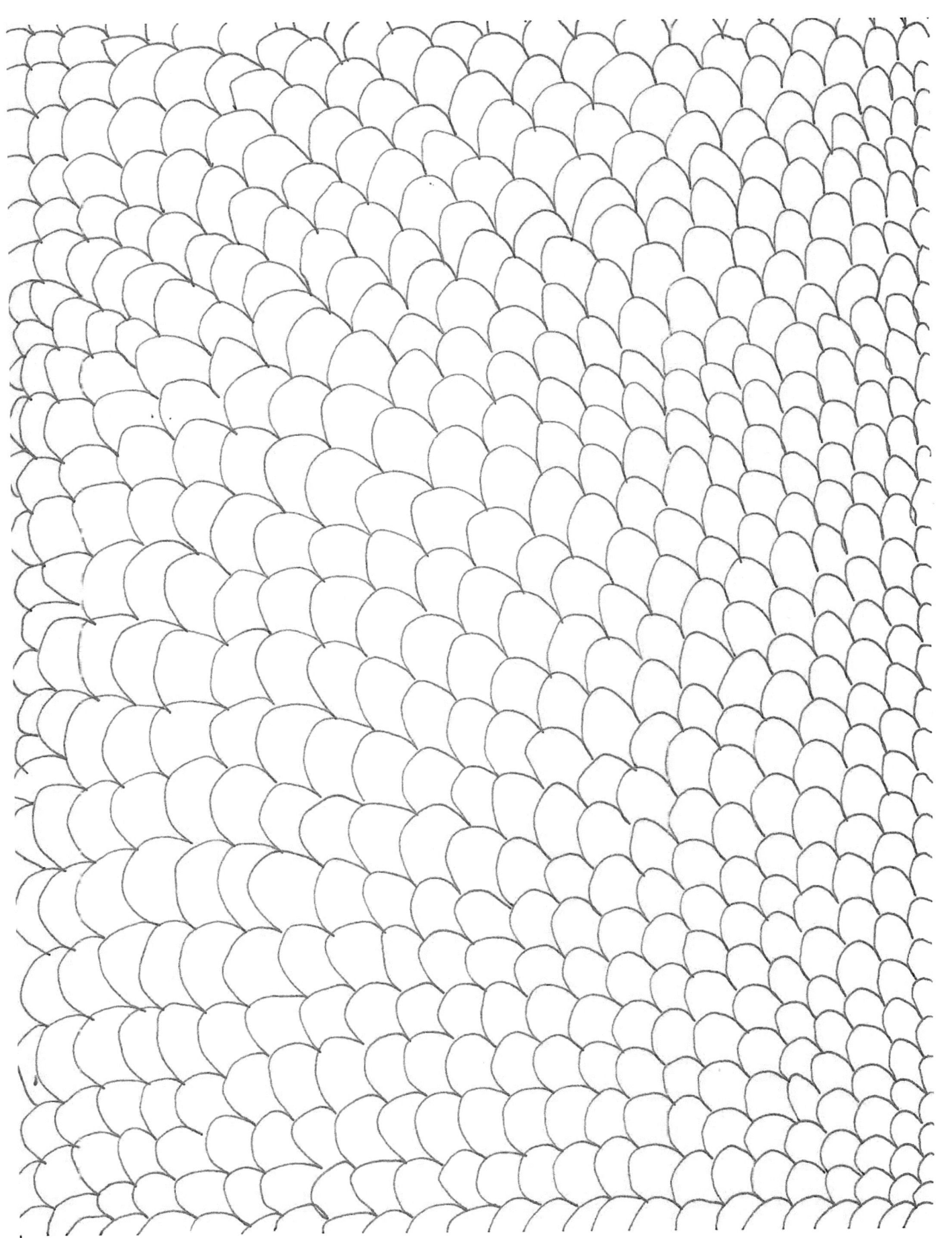

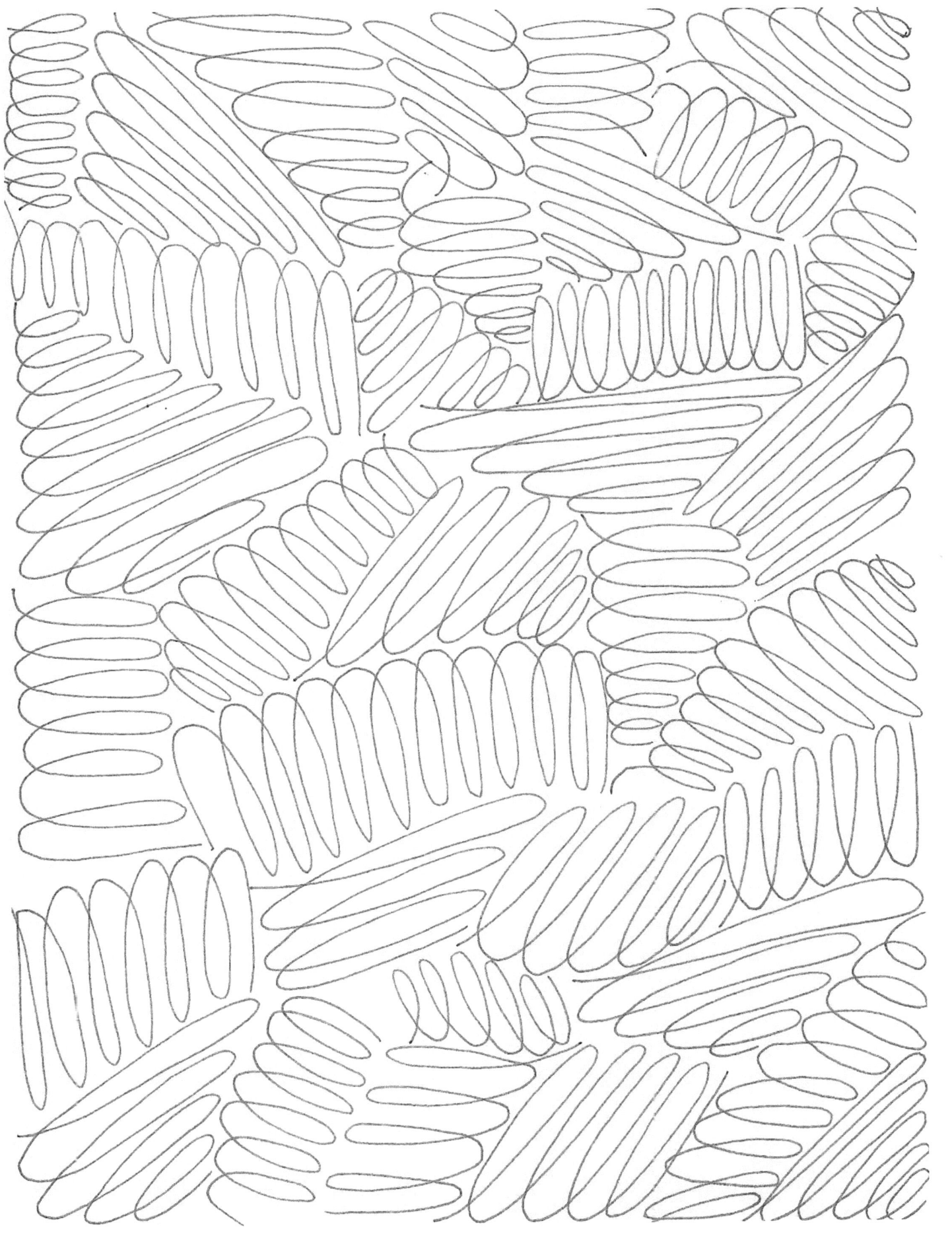

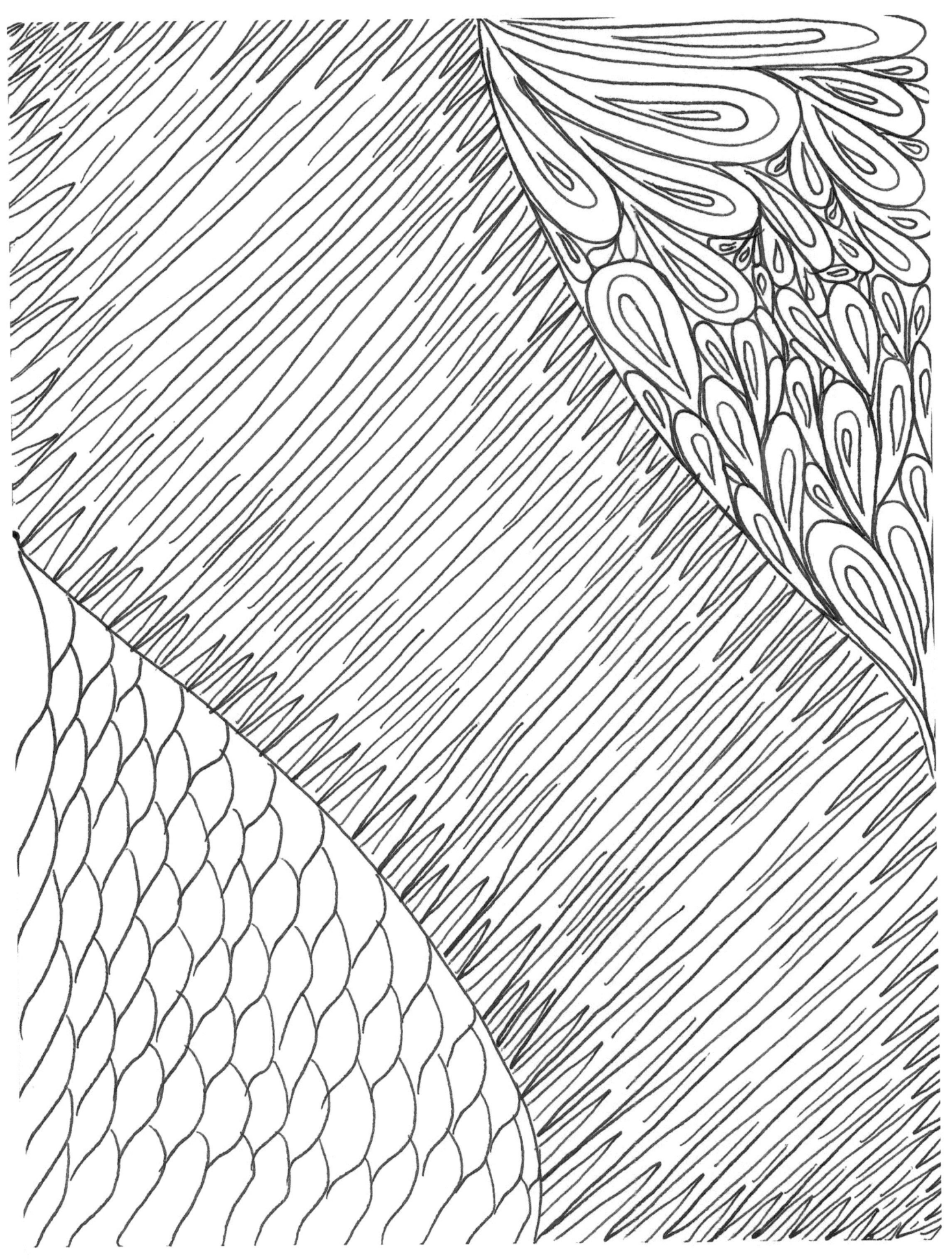

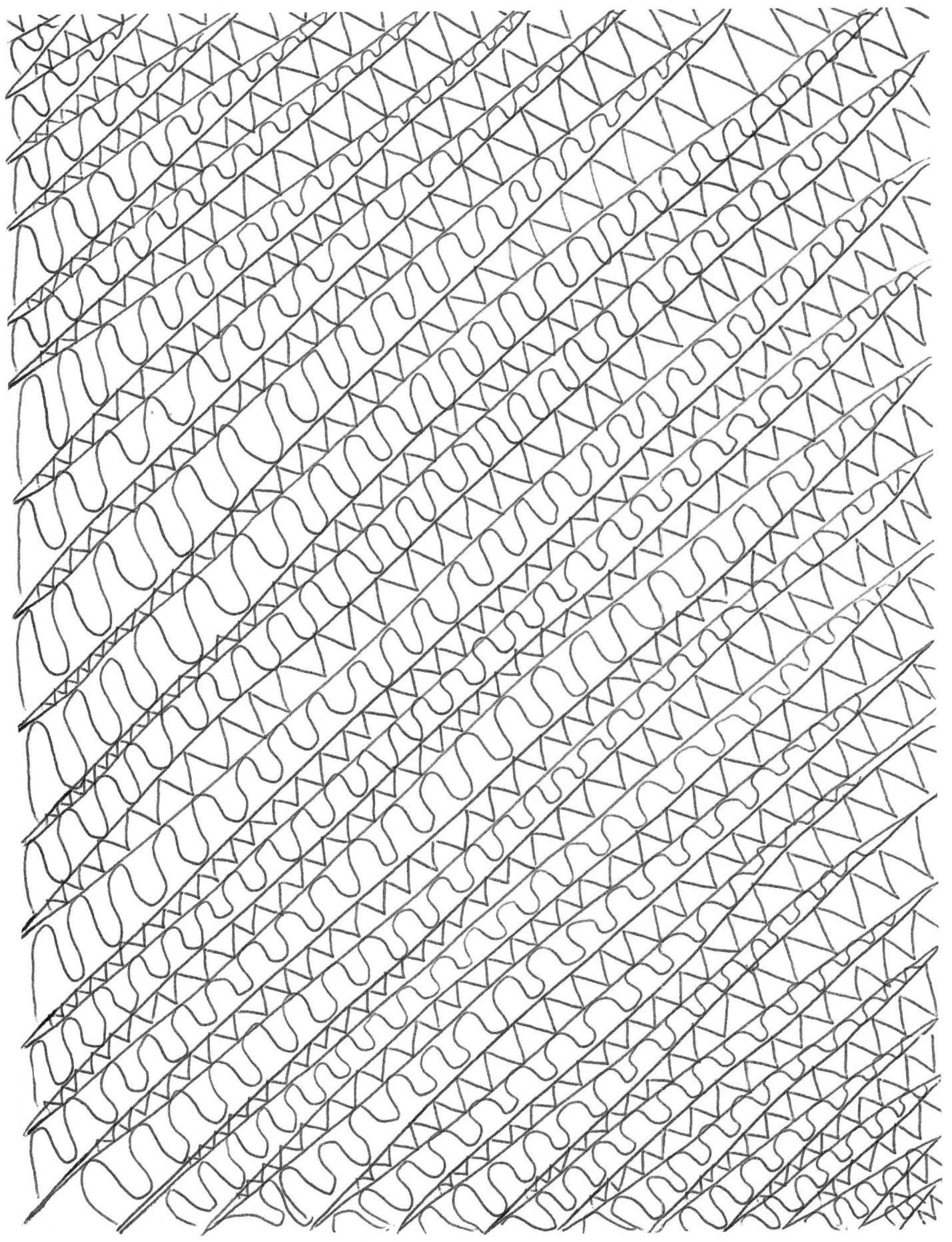

Total Harmony in Hues
Coloring Your Way to Higher Vibrations, Adult Zen

Begin on a transformative journey of self-discovery and relaxation with our captivating coloring book. Immerse yourself in a world of intricate designs and soothing patterns, carefully curated to elevate your spirit and calm your mind.

Key Features:

- **Healing Vibrations:** Engage with lines and patterns designed to resonate with healing vibrations, promoting a sense of balance and tranquility.
- **Mindful Coloring:** Each page serves as a canvas for your creativity, guiding you towards a meditative state where stress dissipates, and serenity takes over.
- **Choose Balancing Colors:** Explore a kaleidoscope of color when you carefully select colors that work in harmony with your vibrations to create a visually pleasing and energetically balanced experience.
- **Holistic Design:** Beyond aesthetics, our designs are strategically crafted to encourage personal growth and introspection, making this more than just a coloring book.
- **Therapeutic Complexity:** Find the perfect balance between complexity and simplicity, catering to both seasoned artists and those new to the therapeutic benefits of coloring.
- **Positive Energy:** Infused with positive energy, each illustration is a tool for mindfulness, encouraging you to rediscover the joy of being in the present moment.
- **Personal Growth:** Use this coloring book as a holistic tool for personal growth, allowing the vibrations of the lines to guide you towards a state of total harmony.

Total Harmony in Hues is not just a coloring book; it's an immersive experience designed to heal, inspire, and promote adult zen. Let the vibrations of the lines guide you on a journey of self-discovery and creative rejuvenation.